Rooted in Adoption

Rooted in Adoption

A COLLECTION OF ADOPTEE REFLECTIONS

VERONICA BREAUX & SHELBY KILGORE

Foreword by Jules Alvarado, MA, LPC

Copyright © 2020 by Veronica Breaux and Shelby Kilgore

ISBN 978-1-09830-362-4 print

ISBN 978-1-09830-363-1 ebook

To adoptees, some of the strongest people with the most beautiful souls. We lost so much, yet we continue to give. Thank you for sharing your experiences with the world.

CONTENTS

Foreword 1

Acknowledgements 6

Introduction 11

It's Complicated 12

Failed 15

Misunderstood 17

Teachable Moments 18

Acceptance 20

Free 22

Opportunity 24

The Man I've Become 25

Twice Blessed 27

Loneliness 28

Adoptee Support 30

Self-Reflection 31

Beautiful 33

The Long Ride Home 35

Family 36

A Second Chance 37

Honesty is the Best Policy 39

Resilience 41

I Am Unique 43

Moving Forward 44

Traumatized 45

Refocusing 48

Identity Development 50

One Big Scar 51

What is Adoption? 53

Grief 55

No Regrets 57

Isolated 59

Inspiration 60

It's Harder Than You Think 62

I Am Worthy 63

Chosen 65

My Adoption Story 67

Opening Doors to the Past 69

Runs in the Family 70

The Hidden Pain 72

A Source of Trauma 74

The Missing Piece 75

Journey of a Lifetime 77

Two Families 79

Where Do I Belong? 80

The Process 82

Déjà Vu 84

Positive Light 86

Late Discovery 88

Adoption on Film 89

Suffering in Silence 91

About the Authors 93

FOREWORD

Why listening to Adoptees Matters:

Adoption is hard.

Adoption is a blessing.

Adoption is the way.

Adoption should be illegal.

All of the above statements are accurate, depending on who is saying it.

Thirty years of service in the adoption field has resulted in a myriad of thoughts, beliefs, emotions, and responses of my own to the experience of buying, selling, and trading kids in America.

I know, that sounds harsh. It is.

But it is also true.

Sitting, holding space, crying, and celebrating with adoptees and adoptive families has been one of the great blessings of the medicine that I come to offer.

Speaking on the experience of adoption around the globe and hearing the voices of the adoptee has been both a gift and an insurmountable amount of pain to which I bear witness on a daily basis.

Working with other professionals and other adoptive parents who give their love, energy, resources, homes, and hearts to our adopted children, who work to offer a chance at a life that many adopted children would not otherwise have, has blessed me. I have seen love pour from the hearts and spirits of adoptive parents, even as they watch their children suffer, move through confusion, rage, anger, blame, and desperation to understand how they could have been given away.

Where there is light, there is also dark.

I am a parent who has raised other parents' children. I hear the cries of those children still, decades later. I know, with no doubt, that no amount of my love will ever, ever replace the love they crave. My love may soothe the rampage for a while, but my role is, at all times, to be drawn as deeply into their experience as they will allow, as I might earn, and as we may co-create until the time they choose to join me in my experience.

The Trauma of Adoption

The experience of the adopted child is often overlooked. We celebrate completing families. We have big adoption parties that fail to realize the devastation, suffering, longing, and primal loss of the child at the center of attention.

When an infant or child is separated from his or her birth mother, it is undeniably traumatic. All of the once-familiar sights, sounds, and sensations are gone, and the infant is placed in a dangerous situation—dangerous that is, as perceived by the infant. The only part of the brain that is fully developed at birth is the brain stem, which regulates the sympathetic nervous system, that is, the fight, flight, or freeze response. The parasympathetic ability to self-soothe is not yet developed. The baby needs his or her familiar mom to act as the soothing agent to help with self-regulation, but she's not there. A stranger has arrived.

Some studies have shown that experiences before age three are encoded as implicit memories and become deeply rooted as life truths, because they occur before the development of language or cognitive understanding. When adoptive parents can be sensitive to this and later help put explicit language to what their child has experienced, they may reduce the long-term manifestation of adoption trauma to some degree. My experience is that few, very few, adoptive parents have any introduction to or understanding of the trauma of adoption, so this necessary healing experience does not occur.

Those of us who grew up with our birth parents simply cannot comprehend the experience of adoption for the adoptee. The most sacred connection has been broken. It might find some healing along the way, but once broken, that connection will remain broken forever.

Adoptees know that only another adoptee really gets it, so they put their emotions, their feelings, and their stories away. They hide them in an effort to protect. A long, heavy, and dark shadow is cast on the voice of the adoptee.

The voice of the adoptee is silenced.

When adoptive parents consider the journey of parenting someone else's child, the most vital step that they can take is to be very, very clear about who they are and why they are adopting.

Are they adopting for themselves or for the child? Who is this really for? Do they understand the trauma of adoption?

Is this an altruistic act of grace and kindness? Is this a gift of family for a child? Can they see the role of parent through the eyes of their adopted child?

Have we done all that we possibly can to reunite this child with biological family and to bring healing to the birthparent-child relationship?

Or is this an attempt to complete you? To fill a void in you that you believe can be relieved through the life of another?

It's a tough, haunting question, I know.

Years of sitting with adopted children and listening to their voices tell the stories of loss, pain, isolation, and confusion that emanate from a deep sense of not belonging, from of the feeling of having no sense of self, have left their voices ringing in my head.

The Voice of the Adoptee

The voice of the adoptee is frequently spoken through behaviors, not words.

The experience of being given away, abandoned, left, or rejected parlays into belief about their worth, their value, and their lacking sense of self.

Behaviors become blanketed in this shame. The need to control some aspect of their life over which they have had no control may explode. Adopted children frequently suffer from lack of self-worth and identity confusion. Many adopted children acclimate in one of two ways: testing every limit in an effort to discover for themselves if they will be abandoned yet again, or struggling to fit in, squeezing into the mold—even to the point of isolation—in hopes they will quietly keep their place in the adoptive family.

The majority of the adopted people who I serve today speak of a false self that they created in an effort to be kept.

The very vulnerable and raw feelings of grief, despair, anger, and fear become the coping mechanisms of both adoptive parent and child. When these feelings become the way parents describe their child's personality and character, they are leaving out the real truth. These behaviors and feelings are the voice of the child in the only language he or she knows.

I teach parents to use curiosity and compassion as they wonder about their child's behavior. I teach parents about the impact of adoption trauma to the brain–body–spirit system.

Few, if any, adoptive parents understand the early, complex experience of being relinquished as a child and that the child is now wired to expect more of the same over the course of their lifetime. Many adopted children unintentionally set themselves up to recreate the abandonment experience, thus fulfilling their own sense of shame and unworthiness.

Many well-intended adoptive parents with whom I work get stuck on the behaviors of their child, not yet willing or ready to understand from the child's perspective. The parents are tired, worn out, and confused. So, too, are the children.

We are complicit in the trauma of adoption if we do not learn to listen to the adoptee in whatever language he or she speaks.

Truth

We will be let down any time that we depend on another person to complete us. Not one person was sent into this lifetime to complete you, to make you happy.

You being happy is up to you. Not your child.

When the behaviors, actions, and words of another control how we feel, we have lost who we are.

If we are not clear about who we are to begin with, we will easily and quickly lose our way.

Adoption is a life-long journey for all involved.

Listening to the adoptee is the most powerful and healing medicine that we might offer.

Just listen.

Be quiet, still, and attentive.

Listen. For them.

But also for you.

Please listen.

Jules Alvarado, MA, LPC
Mamma J to many
Founder/Senior Clinical Consultant,
The Alvarado Consulting Treatment Group
303-431-0604 | juli1@alvaradoconsultinggroup.com
www.alvaradoconsultinggroup.com
9014 Tahoe Lane
Boulder, CO 80301

Jules Alvarado is an internationally recognized author, speaker, and Licensed Professional Counselor. She is also a healing expert in the area of trauma informed care. Her work has been taught in more than 15 countries, and to tens of thousands of people.

ACKNOWLEDGEMENTS

With thanks to Julie Hye Jin Cavanaugh, Valerie E. Knight Naiman, Jillian Zoern, Paige Adams Strickland, Daphne Louise Harling, Mary Moore, Nicki Amouri, Jaynia Batsimm, Ron Carlson, Susan C. Ortiz (birth-name Madelynn), Pernilla Iggstrom, Tammy Murphy, Mei Kelly, Andrea Coston, Erin Nakagaki, Damon L. Davis, Terri Champion, and Wilhelmina Kawaii Cho.

And, of course, to all other adoptees that contributed to this project. Thank you for your courage.

Last but not least, many thanks to Jules Alvarado, who has provided tremendous guidance and support to the adoption community. We love you and are immensely grateful.

Adoption Terminology

Adoptee—Someone who has been adopted.

Adoption—The act of a child being adopted and legally raised by a person or married couple as their own, after the child's birth parents have either passed away or their legal rights as parents have been terminated by choice or by the state/country.

Adoption Fog—Suppressed emotions an adoptee may have regarding their adoption experience. Some adoptees talk about "coming out of the fog" well into the later part of their adulthood.

Adoptive Parent—The mother or father of an adoptee.

Adoption Triad—Consists of the biological parents, adoptee, and adoptive parents.

Amended Birth Certificate—A birth certificate that is altered such that the names of the adoptive parents are listed as the only and sole parents of the adoptee.

Birth Father or First Father—The biological father of the adoptee. First father may also be used.

Birth Mother or First Mother—The biological mother of the adoptee. Many feel the term "birth mother" is outdated and demeans a woman to nothing more than a breeder. Because of this, the term first mother is also used. Both terms mean the same thing.

Birth Parents—The biological parents of an adoptee.

Closed Adoption—When the identities of the birth parents are concealed from adoptive families as well as the adoptee.

Foster Parent—Temporary caregiver for someone waiting to be adopted or to be reunited with one or both birth parents.

Identifying Information—Information that provides the full identify of the birth parents.

International Adoption—An adoption in which the child is adopted by an individual or couple who are nationals of a different country.

Kinship Adoption—An adoption in which a member of the biological family raises the adoptee.

Non-identifying Information—Anonymous information on the adoptee's birth parents and/or family history, which might include ages, ethnicities, talents, and, sometimes, medical information.

Open Adoption—When the identity of the birth family and adoptive parents are shared. No laws are set in place, at either the national or state level, to assure the adoption remains open. Open adoptions sometimes fail, for a variety of reasons.

Original Birth Certificate—An unaltered, true copy of the Certificate of Live Birth, indicating the names and information of the birth parents. In most states, it is illegal for adoptees to access his or her own original birth certificate.

Search Angel—Individuals who volunteer time and experience to help an adoptee locate his or her birth family. Some search angels are retired paralegals, genealogists, or have their own personal connections to adoption.

Semi-Open Adoption—The adoptive family maintains contact with the biological family, usually through a third party, where letters and photos can be exchanged.

Transracial Adoption—The adoption of a child into a family where the adoptive parents are of a different race and/or ethnicity than the adoptee.

*"No one comes to the earth like grass.
We come like trees. We all have roots."*

Maya Angelou

INTRODUCTION

Rooted in Adoption: A Collection of Adoptee Reflections provides an intimate glimpse into the lives of several adopted people. Adoptees have always been told to "be grateful." While some adoptees may feel a sense of gratitude, that does not dismiss feelings for the loss of the biological family. The authors collected insights from adoptees of various ages, ethnicities, and experiences. It is our goal that, you as you read this book, you put aside any preconceived notions you have regarding adoption. We live in a society that tends to publicize the glammed-up, rainbow, sugar-coated, *Annie* persona of the adoption experience, when it is a far more complex issue than most people understand. It has only been within recent years that adoptees have been given a platform. While some of these stories are difficult to read, it is necessary that you not only hear them but also learn from them. Only then can we change the laws that, for decades, have denied us one simple right … the right to know who we are and, in turn, begin the healing that we all deserve. We understand some of the language in this book may be unfamiliar, but a terminology guide has been provided to clarify the meanings. This book should serve as a resource for adoptees, adoptive parents, potential adoptive parents, mental health professionals, and educators. Our hope is that, as you read through these reflections, you get a better understanding of the thoughts and feelings surrounding those who have been adopted.

IT'S COMPLICATED

"The sense of identity provides the ability to experience one's self as something that has continuity and sameness, and to act accordingly."

Erik Erikson

I don't think I truly understood how much adoption affected me until several months ago, when I learned that my birth mother had taken her own life four years previously. That unleashed many years of suppressed emotions.

But looking back, I think about how one of my favorite children's books was *Are You My Mother?* and how I wrote in my Judy Blume diary at age eight that my real mommy was a princess and she was going to come take me away when I was mad at my mom about something. Around the same age, I called my (controlling and cleanliness-obsessed) mother "Mommy Dearest." For a long time, I think Christina Crawford was really the only adoptee I knew about. Though fortunately I was not physically abused, I certainly related to her on some level.

While I always knew I was adopted, it also wasn't something that was really talked about much, and I definitely didn't feel like I could share any difficult feelings about it. My upbringing was mostly okay, but I did always feel like the odd one out. I look nothing like my mom or dad, and I stared at my face in the mirror a lot, from about age seven through my teens. My mom said I was being vain, but I think now that I was trying to figure out who I was, who I looked like. I was taller and dark-haired, with big eyes and full cheeks, a stark contrast to my Scandinavian mother and Irish stepfather. I was a daydreamer and a reader, off in my own little world much of the time. I liked the arts, while my mom and stepdad were very math and logic oriented.

I wrestle with issues of self-image and self-worth to this day, and I think part of that is due to the lack of genetic mirroring, of never seeing myself reflected in those around me. I have struggled with depression for at least twenty years, much more so for the past several years. I have not been actively suicidal, but I have had periods where I just didn't care if I died and did not take good care of my health, leading to problems now. I have a tendency to isolate myself, or test people to see if they will leave me, and I have a hard time holding onto lasting friendships. I chose to estrange myself from my adoptive family for several years.

Growing up, I felt sort of vague and nebulous. I didn't know anything about them at all. I wondered about my birth mother and who she was quite a bit, and though I did sometimes wonder who my birth father might be, he was much less on my mind.

When I was about sixteen or seventeen, my mom told me my birth mother's last name. Every time I had to fill out medical history information and had to write, "unknown — adopted" I felt a twinge of sadness and would wonder. Like so much about being adopted, it's complicated.

My birth mother had not been supported in keeping me, as I eventually discovered. Instead, she was coerced by her own mother into giving me up, an event that affected her deeply for the rest of her life and contributed to her mental health struggles.

I wish it were not a closed adoption. I feel strongly that closed adoption is a moral evil, cutting off vital information and possibilities for connection. It has caused pain for me and so many others.

I am enraged that adoption agencies can get away with charging so much money for what is essentially my own information, and that I'm also not allowed to access the first legal document of my life, my original, unaltered birth certificate.

I wish my birth mother hadn't felt so overwhelmed by the situation that she cut off contact. I wish I had tried reaching out sooner. I wish she knew that I do not blame her for anything, that I feel so much love and empathy for her. I wish more people had been there for her when she needed it.

I can't really regret the life I have, the people I love, the experiences I've had, both good and bad. At the same time, it's so hard not to wonder "what if." What if my birth mother had been supported by her family? What if my birth father had known? What if I'd been able to know them all these years?

It's healing and exciting to be making these connections now to my birth family, but it also fills me with deep sorrow and anger—the very fact that I have to get to know my own father, aunt, cousins, and other relatives. And underlying it all is the grief that I cannot do this with my birth mother. I also feel such sorrow for newborn–me, who was taken from the familiar smells and sounds of her mother, placed in some sort of foster home for two weeks, and then removed again to be adopted.

Ethnicity: White
Gender: Female
Current Age: Forty-four years old
Age of Adoption: Two weeks old
Place of Birth: Wabasha, Minnesota
Closed or Open Adoption: Closed

FAILED

"Family is the most important thing in the world."

Diana, Princess of Wales

My adoption was a painful process that affected my entire life. I was only eighteen months old when social services separated my half-siblings and I into different foster homes. Our biological mother and my biological father had a violent relationship while married and, in addition to my mother's drug abuse and neglect, she was deemed unfit for custody, despite countless efforts toward reunification. Instead, my last foster family adopted me when I was three years old. They were a married couple with two older boys that I grew up to know as my brothers.

Originally, my adoption was open, with a sibling agreement contract and visitation rights for my parents. Somehow, the first contract fell through and I lost contact with my half-siblings and younger full brother. Then, my parents failed to comply with the visitation terms and my mom sent me her last letter when I was only five. I still remember that day, and can still feel the intense emotions of shame, happiness, and loss I felt. She wrote that she'd always be there for me and then vanished, which tore me apart. The reality was that at the age of five, my family vanished from my life without any explanation or goodbye, leaving me with another family that expected me to erase my identity and become a part of theirs. I couldn't voice why I was in so much pain at that age, and started to show signs of behavioral issues in kindergarten. My adoptive family couldn't understand why I was unable to move on, and instead of providing me with their support, they punished me when I struggled and rejected who I was. It only added to my deep scars.

I searched for my lost family my whole life, and found my father's Facebook page when I was in eighth grade. My adoptive parents denied that it was him, and reprimanded me for looking. When I was seventeen, I found my mother's Facebook page. It was both beautiful and extremely painful as I scrolled through proof that she was still out there, and wrote me a post every year on my birthday. This made me feel less abandoned, and I started to understand that my family wanted me back. I knew I had to tell my adoptive parents, but I was terrified of their reaction. My adoptive mother took it unexpectedly well, and even helped me locate my siblings, as well as confirmed that I actually had found my father years ago. Since then, I have slowly begun to reconnect with the family I lost. It has not been easy. A lot of memories and repressed feelings have been brought back to the surface, and there are inconsistencies in my adoption story, which I may not find all the answers to. I still have many reconnections to make, and am currently working to heal my emotional scars.

I have found support through close friends, my biological family, all of my siblings (including my adoptive brothers), and online adoption-support groups. For years I grieved alone, but finally understand that there are people out there who have experienced similar situations and struggles as I have. Strangers and I connect through our understanding of the adoption reality. I fight distrust of people's intentions, anxiety, depression, and other struggles. If I could change my adoption, I'd stop my family's disappearance from my life. I would have grown up understanding my identity and knowing my biological families. Even though my adoptive parents provided me with a home and financial stability, they treated me as though I were a broken object that could never be fixed. I am not broken, but a daughter from three families, and am just beginning to understand who I am.

Ethnicity: Hispanic
Gender: Female
Current Age: Eighteen years old
Age of Adoption: Three years old
Place of Birth: Lawrence, Massachusetts
Closed or Open Adoption: Open (Failed)

MISUNDERSTOOD

"No one would talk much in society if they knew how often they misunderstood others."

Johann Wolfgang von Goethe

I was adopted due to my birth parents being fifteen and sixteen years old. Their parents (my biological grandparents) put me up for adoption. My biological grandparents on Dad's side had no idea. My biological grandfather on my mother's side had more than twenty kids (with multiple women). Growing up I felt misunderstood, out of place, and different—I never knew who I was or where I belonged and was always trying to please everyone else while I suffered. I met my biological family when I was twenty-one years old. My biological mom found me on MySpace. There was a bad ending with my biological mom's side, but a great one with my biological dad's side.

> Ethnicity: White
> Gender: Female
> Current Age: Thirty-two years old
> Age of Adoption: Birth
> Place of Birth: Syracuse, New York
> Closed or Open Adoption: Closed

TEACHABLE MOMENTS

"If you have knowledge, let others light their candles in it."

Margaret Fuller

Adoption has had a huge impact on my life. Even when professionals in the day (the early 1960s) told my adoptive parents to just treat me normally, they had no idea what I would think as I grew and became more aware. Thank goodness my adoptive parents told me what they believed was the truth. Adoption has affected my social life (especially in the early years), because I saw it as a dreadful secret and a personal flaw. I never told peers at school lest I be bullied for it. I was awkward enough. My adoptedness was a veil that separated me from so-called regular people. They knew secrets to life that I might never know. Today, it's great to have been adopted, because I now have met online and real-life adopted friends. I never had an adopted friend until I went to a support group as an adult. Every one of us has a worthy and fascinating story.

As a young person (before receiving my original birth certificate), I thought mainly about my birth mother, but rarely seriously. I thought of her as a mystery person who existed and I knew her in my mind as "The Lady Who Had Me." After my adoptive maternal grandmother died, when I was nineteen, I had a weird hunch that The Lady Who Had Me was also deceased, and on another plane had met my grandma. They knew the secrets to my beginnings, secrets that were forbidden to me still. When I did reunite with my birth family, I found out that my biological mother actually did pass away young. I sensed it years ago. Now that I am in successful reunion with everyone else on both sides, I think about them every day. I have one biological brother and five biological sisters. We never use the prefix half". My adoptive and biological families have become as blended as they possibly can. Holidays can be big, crazy fun.

If I want to discuss adoption, these days I no longer hesitate. I work it into conversations and use the chat as a teachable moment for anyone who has never considered adoption to be a complex situation, especially if you are in reunion. Most people I have met are open and happy to hear what I have to say, even if it alters their original understanding. I also blog and participate in adoption conferences when possible. It's a great way to connect with others in the adoption community.

Ethnicity: White
Gender: Female
Current Age: Fifty-eight years old
Age of adoption: Thirteen months old
Place of Birth: Cincinnati, Ohio
Closed or Open Adoption: Closed

ACCEPTANCE

"We cannot change anything until we accept it."

Carl Jung

My adoptive mum passed away when I was two, so I grew up being raised by my adoptive father. As a child, I always fantasized about what it would be like if my biological family raised me, believing that one day I would find them and we would live happily. I found out at age nine that my grandparents on my birth mother's side adopted me, which was confusing to me at such a young age. My birth mother was also adopted, and I didn't find out about the rest of our biological family for a couple more years. Finding out about my biological family on my mother's side was not what I dreamed of as a child. I found out that they were dangerous people, specifically human traffickers, and it gave me more of a sense of gratefulness toward my adoptive family. I knew that even though I had trauma through adoption, it would have been much worse if I were with that side of my family. Learning this information made me want, more than ever, to find my birth father. When I turned nineteen, I went searching for him. My birth mother refused to tell me his name, so I had to do some digging on my own. Eventually I found out who he was, and I met with him a few times. I found out quite quickly why my birth mother did not want me speaking to him. Suddenly, all of the dreams I had as a child of finding the perfect family were shattered. I knew that wasn't reality. I do not speak to my birth family, or much of my adoptive family aside from a few people, but I've learned to be okay with that now. I no longer long for something I don't have, and am comfortable knowing that everything that happened in my life due to adoption brought me to where I am and helped me become who I am today.

Ethnicity: White
Gender: Female

Current Age: Twenty-one years old
Age of Adoption: Birth
Place of Birth: Ancaster, Ontario, Canada
Closed or Open Adoption: Open (Kinship)

FREE

"Feeling free inside oneself is being free."

Rei Kawakubo

I thank God for the family that chose me. I remember when I asked my adoptive mom about being adopted, she said, "We chose you because you looked like us." It took me fifty-five years to come to understand that. What she meant was, I would look like her side of the family. However, the downside to it is I have a terrible time with rejection. I often ask the question to myself, *Why didn't you want me?* Rejection has always been at the forefront of being adopted, because it has been a catalyst for what has happened to me in other relationships I have tried to sustain. I remember going to school on the bus in Philadelphia, and I would look at women who resembled me, asking the question, *Could she be my mother?* Unfortunately, none of them were.

Mother's Day the year I turned fifty was a turning point in my life, because it was then that I realized I never celebrated the mother who gave me life. So, I made a conscious decision to give props to my birth mother and father on those respective days because without them, I would not be. And then, for my fiftieth birthday, I wanted to pursue finding them. I contacted the orphan's court in the county where I was born and began the arduous process. Every day I waited for the mail, and finally the letter came. It had no name or anything. Just some words on official letterhead. Nothing. What a waste of time and money. I wondered if I would ever be so fortunate as to find them. I guess at this age I probably won't, and that will always haunt me.

I suppose I wouldn't change anything, because I was blessed with some amazing parents and my life has been quite an experience. I wish that before my adoptive parents passed away, they had helped me pursue finding my biological family. While watching a TV show about finding lost loved ones, I contacted the show and the last step for the show was to take an Ancestry DNA test. Much to my surprise, the results are that I'm part African and European, which I find pretty darn cool. I guess that explains my affinity for African and England—after all, I do feel related to the Queen. Hmmm?

How I process my feelings of abandonment and rejection are with my therapist, writing my memoirs, and getting my thoughts on paper. My life has been one heck of a journey. Maybe one day, I will be free!

Ethnicity: Black
Gender: Female
Current Age: Fifty-five years old
Age of Adoption: Four months old
Place of Birth: Philadelphia, Pennsylvania
Closed or Open Adoption: Closed

OPPORTUNITY

"Victory comes from finding opportunities in problems."

Sun Tzu

Adoption means opportunity—opportunity for a life, opportunity for change, opportunity for growth. Despite the negative perception and experience some have of adoption, being given a chance to be raised by someone who wants you is better than not having any opportunity at all.

Ethnicity: Korean
Sex: Male
Current Age: Thirty-three years old
Age of Adoption: Six months old
Place of Birth: Busan, South Korea
Closed or Open Adoption: Closed (International)

THE MAN I'VE BECOME

"I am not what happened to me. I am what I choose to become."

Carl Jung

In my early years, I didn't think my adoption affected me much at all. I grew up well adjusted, with the open knowledge that I was adopted, and open support for a search for my biological relatives if I ever chose to pursue it. I can't think of any way that adoption affected my life until my son, Seth, was born. It was then I realized that he was the first biological relative I had ever known, so his presence ignited my desire to find and hopefully meet more birth relatives. I truly didn't contemplate who my natural family was or where they might be very often before his birth.

I've since located my birth mother, who was working right around the corner from my office in Washington, D.C. I had the good fortune to surprise her at her office on her birthday for our reunion day. We developed an amazing relationship for five years, until she passed away suddenly. Years later I located my biological father through DNA testing, which revealed the identity of a different man than my birth mother named as my biological father. I consider myself lucky that both of my reunions were very positive experiences full of acceptance and love.

I wouldn't change anything about my adoption experience. I'm very thankful for the life I've led and the man I've become as a result of my adoption. It's too challenging for me to imagine being referred to by another first and last name, growing up with different friends and alternative experiences, and ultimately having my son, which set this journey in motion. I'm not sad about my adoption at all, but I recognize that everyone doesn't feel the way that I do. We all have to respect one another's opinions and perspectives on adoption, empathizing with one another in a culture of support with acknowledgement of the trauma.

I'm very fortunate to host the *Who Am I Really?* podcast where I interview adoptees about their journeys through adoption and their attempts to reunite with their biological family members. When I need to talk to another adoptee, I always have a network of people I can turn to who I know truly understand my feelings, as I do theirs.

Ethnicity: Black
Gender: Male
Current Age: Forty-eight years old
Age of Adoption: Three to six months old
Place of Birth: Baltimore, Maryland
Closed or Open Adoption: Closed

TWICE BLESSED

"Family is not an important thing. It's everything."

Michael J. Fox

Adoption has affected my life by giving me multiple loving families. I am in contact with my biological mother and her family and I visit them occasionally. I wouldn't change anything about my adoption. I love where I live, I love both of my families, and I feel like God put me where I needed to be. I feel gratitude toward my adoption, because I am lucky to have two families that love me. As a child, I was less aware of my situation and almost took it for granted, but now I know how unique my adoption is and I'm glad to be in such a good situation. I talk to my adoptive parents about adoption-related things and also to my biological mom to answer any of my questions.

Ethnicity: Black
Gender: Female
Current Age: Fifteen years old
Age of Adoption: Two days old
Place of Birth: Boone, North Carolina
Closed or Open Adoption: Open

LONELINESS

"Loneliness and the feeling of being unwanted is the most terrible poverty."

Mother Teresa

I have always wondered about my "real" mother and family. Who was she? Who were they? All my life I can remember wondering about her, making up fantasies in my mind about who she might be. I could not tell these to anybody. I had to keep this a secret, as I knew this would hurt my other mom and dad. I always felt like I didn't fit in to the family I was raised in and suspected that they felt the same. I felt like I was completely alone in the world. It did not help at all with the shame I was developing. Anyone who grew up in or around Buffalo, New York, knows that all bad kids get sent to Father Bakers/OLV Orphanage, and that's where I came from; therefore, I must be bad! I often wondered if my real mother ever thought about me or wondered where I was.

I was raised in a very emotionally abusive home. With little self-esteem and a great deal of loneliness, I began to use alcohol, drugs, and sex at a young age to compensate and try to feel as though I belonged with a crowd. I was pregnant myself by the time I was sixteen years old, the result of a rape by an older man. I had an abortion out of the fear that my family would either throw me out and I would be homeless and alone, or even worse they would send me to a place like my mother had been sent and I would be forced to give up my child. I thought many times throughout my life that I would rather not have been born than been born and given away. It took me forty-six years to come out of the fog after the passing of my elderly adoptive mother. I reunited with my maternal family and siblings in 2016.

My adoptive mother suffered much trauma due to my relinquishment and our relationship, as well as her relationships with her two other children, reflects this. I have developed a wonderfully close relationship with my half-sister. I communicated maybe three times via email with my natural father, and am now in secondary rejection from him. I don't know if his children, my two half siblings on his side, even know about me yet.

Ethnicity: White
Gender: Female
Current Age: Forty-nine years old
Age of Adoption: Three months old
Place of Birth: Lackawanna, New York
Closed or Open Adoption: Closed

ADOPTEE SUPPORT

"Alone we can do so little; together we can do so much."

Helen Keller

Adoption affected everything; it changed my life. I honestly think that most people who are not adopted will never understand what it is like to be adopted. Words cannot do it justice. You can read all the books about adoption, but they will never show how an adoptee really feels inside. Each adoptee has his or her own story to tell. It is heartbreaking to hear all of the sad and lonely stories that you hear on the internet that so many adoptees are going through very difficult times, even after being adopted more than thirty years, because they can not find the inner peace and comfort about who they really are. Yes, I am blessed. I have a wonderful loving family here in America, and in 2012 I was very fortunate to reunite with my Korean family after forty-three years of separation. In 2020, I'm looking to open a non-profit, for Korean adoptees and others, who can call, FaceTime, or live chat anything they want to talk about. It will be a place where they are free to speak their minds and be the support group for all Korean adoptees and other adoptees in the world. God bless.

Ethnicity: Korean
Gender: Male
Current Age: Fifty-six years old
Age of Adoption: Ten years old
Place of Birth: Busan, South Korea
Closed or Open Adoption: Closed

SELF-REFLECTION

"Our self-image, strongly held, essentially determines what we become."

Maxwell Maltz

I think about my biological family often—wondering who they are, how they are doing, if they ever think about me, and if I have any siblings. Adoption has affected me significantly, and it is a large part of who I am. As an adoptee, I continue to reflect on the person I am and the person I want to be.

Growing up in a predominantly white neighborhood was difficult, even though I tried to assimilate and fit in. During my high school years, I actually felt proud to be Asian and wanted to embrace my ethnicity, my Asian culture. My boyfriend was half Filipino/half Latino, and I saw his pride about his different ethnicities. I had the opportunity to be around other Asians and feel more a part of my ethnicity instead of pushing it away.

I don't have contact with my birth family even though I've tried. It has been disappointing during the search process, and I have dealt with the fact that a reunion might not occur, even though I still have some hope. I have heard at adoption conferences that adoptees have this need to be perfect due to their issues of abandonment and being given up by their biological family. I have always put so much pressure on myself, which can tear me apart—especially when I make mistakes. I worry a lot, I don't want to upset people, and I think too much about things. I've been able to deal with these issues better, however there is definitely room for improvement.

I would not change my life one bit and am proud to be an adoptee. Despite the identity issues I've faced, I know my family is my family. Now that I am a mom, it is beautiful to see my toddler twins with my family, which is very diverse consisting of White, Thai, Black, Mexican, and Chinese roots. I know one day my children will have questions regarding my adoption and why I look different from my parents and the majority of my extended family, but I will say that's the beauty of the makeup of our family. We are a diverse family of all different skin colors and cultures, and that makes us extremely special and proud.

Ethnicity: Korean
Gender: Female
Current Age: Thirty-three years old
Age of Adoption: Three months old
Place of Birth: Taegu, South Korea
Closed or Open Adoption: Closed

BEAUTIFUL

"Beauty begins the moment you decide to be yourself."

Coco Chanel

I have been told that I was three months old when I was found in the streets of Seoul, South Korea, in 1969. I spent two months in an orphanage and three months with a Korean family before I was adopted when I was eight months old. Being adopted has always been a natural part of my life. My mum showed me the magazines from the Korean association when I was little. I identified with the black and white photos of children in it. I grew up in two small towns in Sweden in the safe and peaceful 1970s and 1980s, where there were a handful of other adopted children from Korea and the Philippines. As a child, you want to fit in and look like everyone else. When I was sixteen and seventeen and lived just outside of Stockholm, I started to embrace my ethnicity, embracing that I looked different and felt unique and special instead.

I have to say that I was extremely lucky to grow up with amazing parents. I am especially close to my mother, she is my soul mate, and no one understands me like she does. She has always been very supportive about me learning about my heritage and of my curiosity in trying to find my biological parents. I still don't have any information about who they are. I truly believe that my mother and I were meant to be together, it was not a coincidence. The only thing that makes me a bit sad and not feel fully complete is that I do not know anything about my Korean family. I have done DNA tests and contacted my orphanage without result. I have yet to search actively. My nearest DNA match is a second or third cousin.

I think adoption could be a beautiful thing. I don't believe that your children have to be your own blood in order to love them. If that were the case, we wouldn't marry someone we aren't related to, but only marry within our own family. In my opinion, wanting to have children is ultimately a selfish thing, but you are also helping a child by giving them a chance at a good life when you adopt. But it is very upsetting to now learn that so many children have been abducted and adopted illegally for monetary gain.

Since I was a teenager, when my interest in being adopted increased, I talked openly about it and was happy if I could help newly adoptive parents—especially by reassuring them not to worry too much about their child fitting in.

I am a visual artist now and the subject matter is my cultural heritage—of being Asian on the outside, but metaphorically blond and blue eyed on the inside. I use my own adoption as a platform for exploring cultural identity and hope the viewer will reflect on his or her own background and thereby start to respect the heritages of others.

Ethnicity: Korean
Gender: Female
Current Age: Fifty
Age of Adoption: Eight months
Place of Birth: Seoul, South Korea
Closed or Open Adoption: Closed

THE LONG RIDE HOME

"There's no place like home."

Dorothy, *The Wizard of Oz*

I was five when I was put in foster care and ten when I went to my last foster home, which became my adopted home. Before you go to a home where you get adopted, it's a bus ride for a while, and you have to hang on and try to get that second chance that you need. I remember when I first went to the parents I live with now, I was kind of a brat at the time and I love them now. When I was first adopted, that's when I realized this is my home that I will stay, and that's when I realized I would stay at this home and they would become my parents. I feel most loved with us as a family.

> Ethnicity: White
> Gender: Male
> Current Age: Twenty years old
> Age of Adoption: Twelve years old
> Place of Birth: Marion, Illinois
> Closed or Open Adoption: Open

FAMILY

"Ohana means family. Family means nobody gets left behind or forgotten."

Lilo and Stitch

Adoption means to be put with good people and ones that don't abuse you. Basically, the family we have now. My parents mean everything to me. They are safe, secure, and protective.

Ethnicity: White
Gender: Male
Current Age: Twelve years old
Age of Adoption: Five years old
Place of Birth: Carbondale, Illinois
Closed or Open Adoption: Open

A SECOND CHANCE

"It's a second chance at life for a lot of people. I'm an example of that."

Mike Strauss

Adoption to me is basically having a second chance to live a normal childhood. We were lucky to be adopted at the age that we were, because I do know a girl we fostered who aged out of the system. She's never been adopted, and a lot of the times you know people who want to foster and they're like, "Oh, I'm going to get a cute little kid" and they don't realize that when kids are fourteen or older, they get to the age where they're not going to be adopted. Most of the time the kids know that, so I just think that we were lucky that we were adopted at age eight and five (referring to my biological brother).

My parents basically mean safe, people I can go to when I need help, and they're people who love me so much that they're willing to give up everything. I want to say that I have no anger toward my mother. I love my mom, my biological mom. I love both my moms. I think it's kind of weird and cool to be able to say I have two moms. I am very glad that I still get to stay in contact with my biological mom. I think it's very important that you keep the bond with your biological family, because if you don't keep that bond part of you is basically being torn away and you can't really connect with other people, because of that.

I am proud that I am a foster child. I am proud of being adopted. I am proud of who I am. And I am just happy with the person I have become. I actually see me going into foster care as a blessing, because this is a second chance that not everyone gets to have. If you ever get a chance to actually see what other kids have to go through, kids who don't have the chance that you got to have, kids who were living the nightmare that you were living and have to live it for the rest of their lives, you can see how lucky I was. I realize how much God provided for me and how much luckier I am to live in a country where there is foster care, where people do care about you enough to get you out of a living nightmare.

Ethnicity: White
Gender: Female
Age of Adoption: Eight years old
Current Age: Fifteen years old
Place of Birth: Marion, Illinois
Closed or Open Adoption: Open

HONESTY IS THE BEST POLICY

"Tell the children the truth."

Bob Marley

I find it hard to believe in love and that I am lovable. Being adopted has also prevented me from knowing how to love. Adoption taught me that I do not like dishonesty, and from that I hate telling lies or being lied to. Being adopted makes it hard for me to form emotional attachments with people. The worst part about being adopted is it is very difficult for me to look at myself in the mirror. Every time I see myself, I see an adopted person.

When I was younger, I thought more about my natural family than I do now that I am older. After several occurrences with the birth mother that felt like rejection all over again, I decided not to try and have any kind of relationship with her or any other members of my birth family.

The thing I would change about being adopted is I wish someone had told me that someone loving me is based on my character and personality, not on me being adopted. I wish I was not adopted at all and that I was raised in and with the family I was supposed to instead of feeling like my adopted family are fake relatives and that my life has been a lie.

Yes, being adopted has made me feel extremely sad. I feel as though I lost myself before I could become who I was or how I might have been. As a teenager, I became preoccupied with my adoption and spent a majority of my time spent wondering *why* and *who*. *Why was I given up for adoption and who did it?*

I have two close friends from my childhood who I talk to when I still feel the negative effects from being adopted. Lately, I have been writing down how I feel.

Ethnicity: Black
Gender: Female

Current Age: Fifty-one years old
Age of Adoption: Unknown
Place of Birth: Muncie, Indiana
Closed or Open Adoption: Closed

RESILIENCE

"In order to love who you are, you cannot hate the experiences that shaped you."

Andréa Dykstra

I've learned to rely on myself. I'm a hard worker in everything I do and I am driven. So on the one hand, I can get a lot of work done. On the other hand, I have difficulty relying on others and asking for help. This hinders my ability to emotionally bond with others.

I've thought about my biological family often, what happened and why it happened. As I heal from my emotional wounds, I get to see that I cannot change the past by thinking about it. In fact, I cannot change my past at all. All I can do is be present and see what kind of future I want to create.

Adoption is never going to be a perfect experience. My complaint was that my family was ill-equipped financially and emotionally to give me what I needed. So, if I had a choice in how it would all happen again, I would choose a well-to-do family that was emotionally stable and had the time to give me the individual attention that I needed. But truth be told, that wouldn't fix me either.

I've processed a lot of emotions about my adoption experience. And there has been profound healing that has happened in me since then. As my view of life broadens, I realize that adoption is one of innumerable traumatic experiences that people go through. My ability to empathize with people has been deepened by my experience of adoption. I am glad to be alive and have a future that I can create.

My thoughts about adoption have changed over time. I was living in Korea at a time when people could barely feed themselves, and being biracial did not help my circumstances either. I know that I was not adopted into an ideal situation, but I realize that my parents really cared for me. They did their best to make sure that I was taken care of.

It will never be perfect, because what I want is to fix the past and the past cannot be fixed. I am an adult now and I have the opportunity to live my life as I please in a pretty cool country.

I talk about my adoption to anyone if the moment calls for it. I used to talk to everyone about it when I was a kid, but it's a topic I seldom discuss now because my life is full. There are many topics going around in my head and adoption is just one of them. I'm a musician, healer, and entrepreneur. I've certainly had some vulnerable moments, but I am also strong and resilient as a result of my past. And I can share these thoughts with people around me.

Ethnicity: Biracial (Black/Korean)
Gender: Male
Current Age: Fifty-two years old
Age of Adoption: Nine years old
Place of Birth: Korea
Closed or Open Adoption: Closed (International)

I AM UNIQUE

"Today you are you, that is truer than true. There is no one alive who is you-er than you."

Dr. Seuss, *Happy Birthday to You!*

Adoption has affected my life positively by giving me a reason to embrace my ethnicity, my uniqueness. I think about my biological family, but do not have contact with them and also don't really have any desire to seek them out. I wouldn't want to disrupt their lives, and also do not want to disrupt my own. I wouldn't change anything about my experience, except that I would have invested in my culture sooner. I don't think my view of adoption has changed much over time. I still feel positively about it and embrace the unique story that defines my childhood.

I don't have any audience that I frequently discuss adoption with, but I am excited to start my exploration into a new community to explore adoption.

Ethnicity: Korean
Gender: Female
Current Age: Thirty-seven years old
Age of Adoption: Six months old
Place of Birth: Busan, South Korea
Closed or Open Adoption: Closed (International)

MOVING FORWARD

"When we are no longer able to change a situation, we are challenged to change ourselves."

Victor Frankl

Being adopted and raised in a small, rural white community in Wisconsin significantly affected my life. I eventually realized that I didn't look like anyone in my family except my biological sister who was adopted along with me. Also, it was very hard whenever my doctor asked if I had any history of illness or disease in my family and all I could tell him was that I was adopted. I know I can't change the past, so I just live for the present and the future.

> Ethnicity: Korean
> Gender: Female
> Current Age: Forty-five years old
> Age of Adoption: Six years old
> Place of Birth: South Korea
> Closed or Open Adoption: Closed (International)

TRAUMATIZED

"It could take you years to actually face what has happened. And numerous more to overcome it."

Carol Sides

What I find to be the most fascinating is that I didn't think I had been affected by adoption until I was about forty-eight. Even then I didn't think it was the adoption per se, I thought it was because I had been raised by a narcissistic mother. Almost in passing, a basic stranger suggested that I had attachment issues. Of course, I didn't think that was possible and, in an attempt to prove her wrong with a quick Google search, I discovered it to be true. In fact, it turns out I'm pretty much a poster child for attachment and abandonment issues. Again, I believed it was simply due to my ice-cold, narcissistic mother. Obsessed with trying to learn more about my symptoms and wanting to find some solutions, I finally had to concede that—while my family was very dysfunctional—I was indeed displaying typical relinquishment/adoption trauma.

Looking back with more clarity, I feel as though I was hired for a part and I learned my lines extremely well. In fact, when it came to my adoption, I never veered from the script. Adoption was wonderful. I'm lucky. I was chosen and special. On the other hand, I never felt as though I fit into my family. From the time I was a small child, I joked about how I was the answer to the first-grade handout "what doesn't belong." For decades, I thought that was hilarious. Now I understand that it's actually quite sad. Seeing pregnant women used to make me feel physically ill. I stopped mentioning that to people when they pointed out that that made me weird. Now I understand that I was having anxiety and likely flashbacks to that time in my own life. Bio-mother was in an unwed mothers home, carrying a bastard baby and being ostracized by society. It was clearly a very stressful time for both of us.

At this time in my life, I can honestly say that being relinquished and then adopted has affected every single aspect of my life. I trust no one. I don't let anyone get close. If someone exits my life, I don't really care. I've never been married, never wanted children. I'm fascinated by people who simply love life. Honestly, I would have been just fine not taking this trip around the sun. There was likely some fantasizing about my bio-family. Unfortunately, I have very few memories regarding my childhood, so I can't remember any specifics.

Five years ago, I decided to search and found my entire biological family. Found bio-mom first, and she was kind enough to disclose who my bio-dad was. She and I no longer communicate. She was the victim, not me. And apparently, I'm not grateful enough. However, I do still communicate with my two maternal half brothers. Bio-dad also that any issues I might have had, had nothing to do with me being relinquished/adopted. Adoption is wonderful, don'cha know? It's been a roller coaster ride with him. His other three children and their families want nothing to do with me. Bio-dad insists on regularly telling me about them, though, which really hurts my feelings.

But somehow, I'm the bad guy. Not sure what specifically I would change, but I do know I wouldn't wish it on anybody. And aside from my mother being narcissistic, I actually had a reasonably good adoption. I never wanted for anything material. I showed horses. With that in mind, imagine asking someone: "Would you willingly choose to never, ever see anyone in your family again, for the privilege of showing horses?"

Even after meeting both bio-parents, I still don't feel as though I belong anywhere. There are no thoughts of wishing I had been raised by either of them. It really is a feeling of being an island unto myself. This past June, my flashbacks became more often and more severe, forcing me to finally reach out for help. I've been diagnosed with severe PTSD. Of course, technically it's Complex–PTSD. You know society likes to pretend that women who relinquish their infants for "a better life" are brave and selfless, and should be admired. The reality however is that if any of that were true, why are we kept a secret? If they truly believed that they were doing something wonderful, there would be no shame. But that's not how it is. In fact, I don't believe for half a second that my bio-mother relinquished me to better my life. It was so she could move on with her life, a very selfish act in my opinion. I was adopted into a family that already had four biological sons. My adoptive mother was an adoptee herself, which seems like it would be beneficial, believing that she understood what it was like. Unfortunately, since my mother never acknowledged how her time in an orphanage and subsequent adoption affected her, she was of no help. Her issues remain unresolved and she was and is incapable of loving anyone, including my father and their four sons. I feel as though my emotional disconnect is times two.

Ethnicity: White
Gender: Female
Current Age: Fifty-four years old
Age of Adoption: Five days old
Place of Birth: Southfield, Michigan
Closed or Open Adoption: Closed

REFOCUSING

"Turn your wounds into wisdom."

Oprah Winfrey

Within the last year, I have made a connection with the maternal side of my bio-family by using DNA. A first-cousin and I found each other and, simultaneous to this, a search angel helped piece the rest of the maternal family line/tree together. Before this, I thought about my biological family in a detached way. I had non-identifying information from the Children's Home Society, but while it felt important and useful, it also felt distant, foreign, or not really me, if that makes sense. Finding this part of my family has confirmed all that was written in the paperwork (and much more, of course) and while that was initially exciting, I'm realizing the overall emotional effect so far has felt limited and I think this is related to the overarching impact adoption has had on my life— that I often don't experience emotions as deeply as I'd like, even positive ones—I often feel detached despite wanting to feel deeply. This is also (of course) related to how I was raised by my adoptive parents, who struggled with mirroring emotional openness and connection.

What would I change? My adoptive family experienced the death of one of their children three years before I was born, and this tragic event had immeasurable effects on each person in the family and how my being adopted into this particular family went. In the early 1980s, perhaps the vetting of adoptive families was less comprehensive than now, but for them and for me, I would have changed this aspect of my adoption (that is, greater vetting, connecting them and us to resources for grief recovery).

Related to this, but somewhat overshadowed by the above, a white family adopted me and I am a biracial person who presents and identifies as a person of color (POC). My adoptive family took a color-blind approach, which is most certainly something I would change about my experience. My own racial-identity development has been a long process (it's still going on) and, looking back, I wish this had been a focus of my family.

I am a psychotherapist and, when I began to make contact with my bio-family, I refocused my time in my own therapy to have a place to process what was occurring and what and how I was feeling—this has been immensely helpful. I'm not sad about my adoption or adoptive experience. Perplexed, maybe, wishful for different aspects? Sure. My bio-mother is not open to reunion and I believe she holds the keys to finding my biological father, so this is painful; it feels abusive and selfish, but I don't have control over that.

Ethnicity: Biracial (Black/White)
Gender: Female
Current Age: Thirty-nine years old
Age of Adoption: Three days old
Place of Birth: Orlando, Florida
Closed or Open Adoption: Closed (Transracial)

IDENTITY DEVELOPMENT

"In all of us there is a hunger, marrow deep, to know our heritage—to know who we are, and where we have come from. Without this enriching knowledge, there is a hollow yearning. No matter what our attainments in life, there is ... the most disquieting loneliness."

Alex Haley

Adoption didn't make a really big impact on my mindset until high school. Obviously, adoption changed my life, because I'm not in China growing up in an orphanage. I don't really think much about my birth family. It's almost impossible to contact my birth family, because at the time it was an illegal act to abandon children in China. I found out that I wasn't part of an adoption community until high school (my senior year). I can talk to other people in the community or my therapist. I don't ever feel sad about my adoption. I know that my life is much better than it could have been in China. I do wish I could have had my birth mom's health records. It is something important to know for my future. I think it's important to be part of the adoption community. I didn't realize how much adoption affects my life. I think I would do work in adoption research or with adoptees in the future. I hope that young adoptees know that they are part of a larger community and that identity development is a lifelong process.

Ethnicity: Chinese
Gender: Female
Current Age: Twenty-two years old
Age of Adoption: Nine months old
Place of Birth: Jiangmen, Guangdong Province, China
Closed or Open Adoption: Closed (International)

ONE BIG SCAR

"It has been said, 'time heals all wounds.' ... The wounds remain. In time, the mind, protecting its sanity, covers them with scar tissue and the pain lessens. But it is never gone."

Rose Kennedy

After years, I finally found peace with my loss. Adoption is one big scar that, in my opinion, every adoptee must give a place in his or her life. It's a journey we, as adoptees, must make. Some make it early in life, others later or never.

My search for my birth parents started very early in my life. I've never had the feeling that I fit in. I've searched a long time for my place in this world. This year my search ended. I now know that my home is still my birth country, South Korea. My home will never be my adoptive country. Sadly, due to circumstances, I can't move, but keeping in touch with other adopted Koreans helps soften my homesickness. My best friend is in a unique position. She has an adopted brother, and through me, she understands him better. And because of him, she understands me better. From her I get a different view on adoption matters.

When I was a child, I thought of adoption as something to save a child. In time, when I learned more and more about my own adoption, all the mixed-up emotions, and especially the downs in my life, I changed my vision on adoption. I will never recommend adoption. My adoptive mother told me once: "I would never have adopted you if I knew then what I know now about adoption and the emotional scar it left on you."

My adoptive parents were always supportive of my search for my birth parents. They always wanted to be involved with it. Last summer, when I finally made the trip home, my adoptive father traveled with me to meet with my birth father's family for the first time. I've been to Korea now for the third time and every time the plane left the airport toward Seoul, I felt like I was going home. That feeling overwhelmed me the first time. This time I was more prepared, but it hit me just as hard as the first time. When I walked through Seoul, I felt like I belonged there and not on the other side of the world. Meeting my aunts and my grandma did so much to me. They let me feel welcome and wanted.

Seeing my grandma at the place where my father rests was another closure for me. She kept complaining to him that he never saw me back in South Korea after all those years of missing me. We cried together for a time. My birth father passed away in 2016, and I'm the only child with a picture next to the urn with his ashes. That was so surprising and heartwarming. They thought about me when he passed away. I know he had two other sons, my half-brothers, but there's no picture of them there. That instant, I wrote a note to my father and left it there. I've found peace with never seeing him in person and having him answer my questions.

My search isn't over yet. I've done a DNA test to search for my mother, so that will be a new chapter in my life. In my heart, I'm very scared of what I will find. I do know that I can't live the rest of my life in South Korea. I won't fit in there, either. My aunt told me to keep living in my adoptive country, because it's much better than the Korean system. My heart, though, will always stay in South Korea.

Ethnicity: Korean
Gender: Female
Current age: Thirty-nine
Age of adoption: Twenty-two months
Place of Birth: Seoul, South Korea
Closed or open adoption: Closed (International)

WHAT IS ADOPTION?

"I say to everybody, 'Adoption is not for the faint of heart.'"

Mariska Hargitay

For me, adoption is a way for childless people to receive a child and an orphan to get guardians. The idea is nice, but not always successful for those who are involved.

The many difficult separations that I was exposed to at an early age left their mark on me: I do not trust anyone, I have low self-esteem, and I try to avoid separation from people close to me.

Adoption meant that I looked different. My adoptive parents told me that I was adopted because my mother was very young and poor and couldn't take care of me.

I know now that this was something they invented, because nobody knows where I came from, or why. I know now that I was found on the street when I was around one year old.

The most difficult thing is my self-image. *Who am I? What am I doing here and why?*

My relationships with other people are complicated and, despite years of therapy, it doesn't seem possible to get some peace.

"You should be grateful that you came here. You would have lived on the street otherwise," is not a question, but a statement that has plagued me, as if I should be grateful for something people assume.

The most annoying question I constantly get from medical practitioners is probably if there are any diseases in my family. But they couldn't know that I am adopted. Or could they?

If you are not confident in yourself, then you cannot be a source of safety for a child, and especially not a child who has been exposed to traumatic experiences at an early age.

Dare to show emotions, be there as support, listen, talk, and explain. Confirm the child's feelings and thoughts. Introduce the culture and customs of the birth country to the child from the beginning. Be interested in and travel back with the child to the country of birth, if possible. If the child later wants to seek their roots, help them! Above all, if you are not able to show love and care, you are the completely wrong person to adopt.

Ethnicity: Korean
Gender: Female
Current age: Thirty-nine years old
Age of adoption: About age two
Place of Birth: Daegu, South Korea
Closed or open adoption: Closed (International)

GRIEF

"We never truly 'get over' a loss, but we can move forward and evolve from it."

Elizabeth Berrien

There are many things that people do not tell you about adoption. The brochures and pamphlets encourage adoption because babies and children need homes. The advertisements say become foster parents because kids need a home ... but the stories of the adoptees go unheard most of the time. My twin brother and I were fostered and adopted together, which I am thankful for. However, I cannot speak on his experience so this will just be about me! I did not realize how much my adoption affected me until I found myself in therapy at age twenty-four. By this time I had met in person all of my biological family, including my birth mother and biological father. I knew they story of my adoption and I tried to get my original records, but was told they are sealed. I was dealing with the turmoil of being in between my biological family and my adoptive family. I had to heal from my traumatic past as an adult. I never deemed my past as traumatic. I just thought that things were how they were, but it affected me mentally and if has affected my relationship with people, both platonically and intimately. I think about my biological family all the time. I love my birth mother and my biological siblings. I pray for their well-being daily. I try to keep in contact with my biological siblings daily and my birth mother monthly, if possible. I see extended biological family during family reunions.

I would change a few things about my adoption experience. I would not change anything about my experience, because I did as I felt was necessary to find and be in contact with my biological family and I deserved that. Yes, it was challenging and tedious and I did not have the support of my adoptive family until later on in my journey, but I would not do it any other way. Grief is always present. I lost my biological mother. She could not be in my life the way she was supposed to be, and that is an incredible loss. I see her out and about daily, and the hurt and sadness I feel is sometimes unbearable, but I manage. I talk to people who get it. I write a blog about the ups and downs that I deal with on my journey and the support I receive is amazing!

Ethnicity: Black
Gender: Female
Current Age: Twenty-seven years old
Age of Adoption: Seven years old
Place of Birth: Charlottesville, Virginia
Closed or Open Adoption: Open

NO REGRETS

"Great difficulties may be surmounted by patience and perseverance."

Abigail Adams

I was adopted when I was seven months old and came home on Christmas Eve in 1998. My adoption was never hidden from me by my parents and was kind of hard not to notice, considering they were both of Irish descent with big features and fair skin. I don't think I ever would have known I looked so vastly different from everyone else if my classmates in preschool hadn't pointed it out by pulling their eyes to the side. I usually forget I'm even Asian, until I hear a joke or look in the mirror. I hear comments about my "real family," which Korea I came from, and "Your English is great!" a lot. While most aren't malicious as I've gotten older, they are still ignorant to me, but I try to educate when I can. Growing up, my parents made sure to incorporate my Korean heritage in my life. They brought me to Korean adoptee culture camps, celebrated my coming home day, bought me beautiful hanboks, and even, when I was a baby, had a Dol Jabi ceremony for me (I picked the coins). I think the earliest memory of feeling what adoption meant to me was when I went back to my birthplace in 2012. That was an amazing experience, and I felt like I was finally at home. It was like my whole body relaxed subconsciously, knowing I was finally surrounded by people who looked just like me, and for once, it was my parents who stood out. Being adopted has never been easy. I was always very thankful toward my birth mother, and her decision to give me a better life, but there was always a little bit of resentment lingering in the back of my heart. *Why did she give me up, did she not want me?* My parents constantly made sure to reassure me, and while they didn't have the answers I needed, I knew that I was loved and wanted by them. In 2018, I decided to attempt to reach out to my birth mother. After a few months, I received a letter from her, which had pictures of her and her little family. I now know that I have two younger half siblings and a stepfather. She has been very open in wanting to learn more about me, and I have been so grateful for that. I've always known that I wanted to go back to Korea to teach, and maybe in the future, arrangements to meet can be discussed, but for now, I'm finally content having a lot of my twenty-one-year-old questions answered. While I know that everyone has a different adoption experience, I've chosen to grow from mine. I will forever be grateful toward my birth mother and her decision to give me a better life. My family here will never know how much I love and appreciate them for everything they have done for me. I choose to love, experience my life as a proud Korean adoptee, and do my best to make my family proud. I refuse to live with regrets.

Ethnicity: Korean
Gender: Female
Current Age: Twenty-one years old
Age of Adoption: Seven months old
Place of Birth: Pyeongtaek, South Korea
Closed or Open Adoption: Closed (International)

ISOLATED

"It is an absolute human certainty that no one can know his own beauty or perceive a sense of his own worth until it has been reflected back to him in the mirror of another loving, caring human being."

John Joseph Powell, *The Secret of Staying in Love*

I was never allowed to discuss adoption. Adoption caused bonding and trust issues. I have the right to know.

Ethnicity: White
Gender: Female
Current Age: Sixty-nine years old
Age of Adoption: Birth
Place of Birth: Miami, Florida
Closed or Open Adoption: Closed

INSPIRATION

"Instead of letting your hardships and failures discourage or exhaust you, let them inspire you."

Michelle Obama

Adoption is inspiration. I have felt this since an adolescent. The profound mystery that surrounds and haunts closed adoptions hints at the deepest mystery of all—where did we come from and who did we come from? As someone who is alive and who has been given life by not one, but three mothers, these are the questions I must ask. In my mind, I do not separate the object of my thinking as God or my first mother. They are one and the same. I think on them both. I cannot be adopted without being religious, and I cannot be religious without being adopted.

The following are reflections of my graduate school years at Union Geological Seminary:

She is the mystery in me, and the mystery is so deep it cannot be explained but is a feeling, a feeling of trying to recall a memory that has been lost.

I no longer have the memory, but I know it was once there. All I have is this feeling, a very strong feeling, that something was once there but is now gone.

No—it is not gone—it lingers. It is not fully lost. I am trying to get at it, but I do not know what I am searching for. I am just searching. I have no proof that what I am searching for really exists. I only have this feeling—this feeling that I forgot—this feeling that I should remember.

I know I am not crazy. I know the memory exists.

The memory of what?

The beginning of time. Being born. Seeing you for the first time.

What I have lost or forgotten may be huge, but what I do not know, I am not supposed to know. I am only to know that one day all will be revealed. One day, I will know what to call you. One day, I will know your name.

It is a miracle that we have even been left with remembrance and remnants of this memory. The truth we know and have is this: We once experienced something incredibly profound. It dwelled in us. It affected us. It changed us. It became a part of us. We knew it well. We loved it. Then, perhaps suddenly, it left us. We forgot or were made to forget all of this happening—except, that, as it left we cried out in anguish and experienced life-changing panic, guilt, anxiety, grief, and loneliness.

If we are sure of anything, it is we are sure of what we felt. Our crying out is our knowing something was there. Our crying out is the legacy we try to remember. Our crying out is our evidence, our reassurance, of Her.

Ethnicity: Korean
Gender: Female
Current Age: Thirty-two years old
Age of Adoption: Four months old
Place of Birth: Seoul, South Korea
Closed or Open Adoption: Closed (International)

IT'S HARDER THAN YOU THINK

"Hardships often prepare ordinary people for an extraordinary destiny."

Christopher Markus, Stephen McFeely, and Michael Petroni, *The Voyage of the Dawn Treader*

Being adopted affected me with others, because I felt different and I felt like I did not matter. Adoption felt like I was getting taken away from everything I loved and cared for. The most difficult part of being adopted was being separated from my brothers. The most annoying question that I have been asked is "Who do you live with, or do you even live with someone?" I don't think parents should treat their adopted kids differently. Adoption has been a very hard thing for me; it comes with bad things and good things. The bad things are feeling like you don't fit in, feeling different, or people treating you differently. Sometimes you may just feel like crying or screaming. But the good things are that some people show you love with hugs and kisses, affections, and kindness, and give you joy. It's okay to feel all of these things sometimes, but that if anyone treats you differently you stand up and say, "I'm not different. I am the same as you. We are both human beings and we both have feelings and even if we don't have the same background we are still people and deserve a good life, no matter what." Additionally, adoption has been hard, but you can get through it with your new family.

Ethnicity: Hispanic
Gender: Female
Current Age: Ten years old
Age of Adoption: Four years old
Place of Birth: Stockton, California
Closed or Open Adoption: Closed

I AM WORTHY

"Love yourself. Be clear on how you want to be treated. Know your worth. Always."

Maryam Hasnaa

I am twenty-six years old, and was adopted from Warsaw, Poland, at the age of nine. I was in and out of orphanages ever since I was seven years old up to the day that I was adopted. My adoption was not the greatest. I was adopted into an abusive and neglectful home. I have always been searching for something, but being an unloved child, I didn't know what it was that I was missing. As I got older, that longing for love grew stronger. I wanted so much to be loved and accepted for who I was, but in my adoptive family that was nowhere to be found. My parents have, as I mentioned, already brought me a lot of grief. I never felt like I fit in. I felt like I was adopted just to be used for housework and not really adopted to be loved as a child ought to be loved. I remember often spending time outside in the snow on the bench at my bus stop because I wasn't allowed to come inside. And when I was inside, I was locked up and not allowed any interaction with the rest of my family. I would often be given cereal that my adoptive parents knew I didn't like and when I didn't eat it, it would become my next meal. So, I soon began stealing from work because of how hungry I was. I was also often beaten black and blue as a child. Everyone thought my parents were great, but if they took a moment to just look past the fake smile on my face and look into my eyes, they would have seen pain, a story full of unbearable pain. I have been struggling with mental health for as long as I can remember as a result of being put up for adoption and have many times thought to myself, *Why didn't my mom just abort me?* That is a thought that even now I struggle with. Thanks to my treatment team here in the United States, I am regaining my life. I can't fix what happened to me, but I can learn to live on and not let the daily struggles define me. I am wanted,

I am needed, and, most importantly, I am loved. It took the suicides of my friends to realize the worth of my life. I never imagined that my life would be the way it is now. I am finally happy in my own skin. I am happy being who I am. And no one can dictate my worth. No one. Only I can define that.

Ethnicity: White
Gender: Female
Current Age: Twenty-six years old
Age of Adoption: Nine years old
Place of Birth: Warsaw, Poland
Closed or Open Adoption: Closed

CHOSEN

"You're worthy of being chosen, fought for, and loved. Remember that."

Mark Groves

I lived most of my life in a shadow, cast by my birth mother' past. I chose to stay there, to try and undo the hurt she endured being pregnant with me, by trying to redo her story with my own life. Maybe if I could somehow redo her tragedy, she would find peace and I would live a fulfilled life knowing I didn't waste her sacrifices.

So, here's what really happened: In my early teens I repeated history. I watched one too many romantic comedies, fantasized about being sought after by the boy next door, and found myself in a never-ending string of empty relationships until I was twenty-four, all the while struggling with self-love and acceptance. I wrote my own tragedy.

And here's what I came out with on the other side. I'm now thirty, happily married, blessed with my first daughter, and my birth mother passed away a year and a half ago from breast cancer. I lived to mend her, and ultimately it was out of my hands to begin with.

The day after her death was the day I was reborn. I realized that while I felt guilty for being alive, for so long I missed the most important reason for my adoption.

I was chosen! I wasn't a punishment, I wasn't a mistake, I wasn't given up. I was chosen!

Your purpose is what you were born with, not what you were born into. You were chosen for a special purpose that only you will understand, and you should never feel guilty for wanting to live your best life possible. You were chosen for a family that was meant to have you in their lives and, quite honestly, that is sometimes the best purpose of all. You complete an incomplete family—you are what is missing. Never forget that from whatever situation you came, you were always meant for more.

Being adopted used to be the subject I avoided. Now it is my identifier. Don't be afraid to stand out.

Ethnicity: White
Gender: Female
Current Age: Twenty-nine years old
Age of Adoption: Two weeks old
Place of Birth: Springfield, Illinois
Closed or Open Adoption: Open

MY ADOPTION STORY

"I see now how owning our story and loving ourselves through that process is the bravest thing that we will ever do."

Brené Brown

I feel adoption has negatively affected my mental health for my entire life. When I was two years old, my adopted parents divorced and I never saw my adopted father again. I think it was shortly after that when the abuse started. I don't remember a time where I didn't know I was adopted. I was reminded constantly, told that if I didn't do what I was told, I would be "sent back to the orphanage," which I was assured was far worse than the abuse I had to endure every day. I was always told how useless I was, and to this day, even with my accomplishments, I still feel that way. When I was very young, my adoptive mother dressed me up in girl's clothes, put a wig on me, and took a picture. A few years later, she showed me the photo, telling me it was my sister, and she was sent back to the orphanage because she complained too much and didn't do her chores well or fast enough. And the same would happen to me if I didn't do what I was told. I was seven at the time.

I found my birth mother three years ago, and flew from Massachusetts to Texas to meet her. It was the first time since the birth of my son that I felt like I had family. I haven't told her about the abuse, because she honestly felt that she did the right thing letting them adopt me, and I don't want to upset her that much. I feel that there needs to be systems in place to observe adoptees, to make sure they are in safe, abuse-free homes. I belong to a few adult adoptee groups on Facebook, and the number of physically, emotionally, and sexually abused adoptees angers me to no end. And those are just the small percentage of adoptees who feel comfortable divulging their feelings and experiences. Couples looking to adopt need to figure out why they want to adopt. Adoption should be about finding a home for the child, not an attempt to fill an emotional void for the couple. And certainly not about getting free labor, a punching bag, or worse.

I wish my adopted parents had been able to conceive, or had gone a different direction. Neither of them was ready or mentally stable enough for a child, biological or otherwise. Thank you for reading.

Ethnicity: White
Gender: Male
Current Age: Forty-seven years old
Age of Adoption: Two days old
Place of Birth: El Paso, Texas
Closed or Open Adoption: Open

OPENING DOORS TO THE PAST

"Don't give up. Normally it is the last key on the ring which opens the door."

Paulo Coelho

I was adopted when I was three days old, but I didn't know or realize how much it had affected my whole life until I was thirty-seven. The same week my son went away to college and my daughter started kindergarten, I got a close match on a DNA registry website. The next two weeks were full of deep emotions, doors I wasn't sure if I should open or not, and answers to questions I had always asked and never gotten answers to. I never really had anyone to talk to about being adopted. My own adoptive parents acknowledged it and celebrated it, but never answered questions or helped me look for my biological family. When I found them earlier this year, I found out that my biological mother is dead. Doors slammed in my face. So was my dad. Another door. But then I found I had two younger siblings. A door opened. If only it had opened earlier!

That's one thing I would like to change. It's not always roses and sunshine. If I could change another, my mother would have been able to support me with resources she could count on. I am traumatized from adoption. I believe all adopted children are traumatized, whether they realize it or acknowledge it (or not). Adoption rules and regulations need to change. We as a global society need to acknowledge the damage adoption will do.

Ethnicity: White
Gender: Nonbinary
Current Age: Thirty-eight years old
Age of Adoption: Three days old
Place of Birth: Charleston, South Carolina
Closed or Open Adoption: Closed

RUNS IN THE FAMILY

"Adoption has been a part of my life and a part of my family, so it was how I wanted to start. It felt natural and right to me."

Katherine Heigl

I am proud that I was adopted, grateful that my birth mother loved me enough to choose to give me life rather than abort me, even though I was an inconvenience at the time. My (adoptive) mother did such a good job of explaining that I was wanted and hand picked that I went to kindergarten, found out other kids were not adopted, and told them that they might have been a mistake! Luckily, I soon learned that not being adopted did not automatically make someone a mistake. My sister was adopted, my cousin adopted two children, and I adopted my daughter. Adoption sort of runs in the family. Because of my positive experience with adoption, it was always my plan A for having children. Growing up, some of the most frustrating and invalidating things I heard from others were:

1. I needed to find my real family, as if the family I had lived with from birth was not real.
2. I needed to call my biologically related family my first family.
3. Adoption always involves trauma.
4. No one is complete without connections to their biologically related family.

I respect that others have negative or mixed experiences with adoption, and I need to remain open about whatever my daughter's experience may turn out to be. My adoption and my daughter's adoption were God's gifts to me.

Ethnicity: White
Gender: Female
Current Age: Thirty-seven years old

Age of Adoption: Birth
Place of Birth: San Diego, California
Closed or Open Adoption: Semi-Open Adoption

THE HIDDEN PAIN

"The hardest thing of all is when pain is hidden behind a mask of calm."

Sergei Lukyanenko

I have started telling people that I think I am truly one of the lucky ones. This is usually in response to people saying "Wow, you sure were lucky" or "Isn't that amazing, aren't you glad?" Yes, truly. I love my family and fully believe that if I ever reunite with my birth family I will not feel the same connection. The connection that I have with my family took twenty-three years to build, and survived middle school, puberty, and prom. That has been filled with so much love that I could feel confident to venture back to my motherland and try to learn about my culture. Yes, I was truly lucky. My family never hid my adoption from me, never made me feel out of place in our family, always wanted to hear my thoughts and opinions about being adopted, and supported me even after I became a legal adult. Again, I was so, so lucky. When I was younger, I thought that every adopted child had the same life as me, was happy and comfortable. It was not until I got to college that I truly understood that every adoptee has a different relationship with his or her parents. Yes, some are similar, but there is always one thing different that every new adoptive parent can't account for in their books, their chat rooms, or their neighbors. I realized in college that even my close adoptee friends, who brought so much light into my life, were hurt in some way by their adoptive families. I look back into my own life and fail to pick out instances that I felt hurt or targeted by my parents, a biased view but I believe is true. It hurts me to see that so many of my loved ones were confused and angry about their adoption and I, being of the same circumstances, could not relate to them. This confusion, along with a number of conflicts in my life, led me to fall victim to the depression that plagues so many of my adopted brothers and sisters. Me, with my happy life, with parents so perfect and helpful, became another hurt adoptee. As I learn, grow, and heal, I wish I could go back and tell my younger self that even though I have this perfect life and that thousands of adoptees were put in families that were not good or were not the right fit, it is okay to feel pain. And to families hoping to adopt children, you can do everything right, but your child could still feel this pain. Please support them instead of trying to fix them.

Ethnicity: Korean
Gender: Female
Current Age: Twenty-three years old
Age of Adoption: Six months old
Place of Birth: Kyangsan, South Korea
Closed or Open Adoption: Closed (International)

A SOURCE OF TRAUMA

"Adoption loss is the only trauma in the world where the victims are expected by the whole of society to be grateful."

Reverend Keith C. Griffith

The older I get, the more I realize the impact of my adoption on my life. I used to think of my adoption as a time-limited event that happened the day I was born, and then I went on to live my life just like anyone else. Now I see my adoption like a drop of dye. It entered my life at one moment in mine, yes, but it changed the color of everything I experience. When I became a mother myself, and had my own biological child, I became aware.

Adoption used to be the thing that made me special and unique. It was my party trick, the story I told that I knew people would find fascinating. I think I felt that way because I grew up hearing my parents share my story, seeing everyone's responses, and enjoying the attention. Now, I see my adoption as a source of trauma. I think that as a practice, it is terribly flawed. At its best, adoption is merely making the best out of a bad situation. Adoption is the word that captures both the trauma I experienced as an infant being separated from my familiar mother, as well as the provision and love I received in the family that I call home. It is too simplistic to call it love or beautiful.

Ethnicity: Biracial (Chinese/White)
Gender: Female
Current Age: Thirty-five years old
Age of Adoption: One day old
Place of Birth: Tillamook, Oregon
Closed or Open Adoption: Open (Kinship)

THE MISSING PIECE

"There is no greater agony than bearing an untold story inside you."

Maya Angelou

My definition of adoption has changed dramatically over the past fifty-seven years. If you had asked me before third grade, I would have told you that being adopted meant that I was chosen and my parents weren't stuck with me, like they were with my two brothers. In the third grade, we were given the assignment to write our autobiography and it needed to include our birth story such as date, time, and place. It wasn't a secret that I was adopted, and I knew that my mom didn't have these answers. I had read and re-read the non-identifying information that she was given about me, time and again. So, I wrote my assignment and made up the information. When the teacher realized that I had made up the information, my view on adoption changed. I was now different from my friends. This really made the longing for my first parents even stronger. I was certain that they would come get me and take me home with them. My non-identifying information said that they planned to marry, and my child brain felt that as soon as they married they would be back to get me. I think I held onto that dream until I was about twelve. Over the years, there was always a hole, a piece missing, and I knew that it was because I was adopted. For years, I was very angry that I wasn't allowed to know who my parents were. While adoption was not a forbidden topic, I was admonished to be careful in searching because "More than likely, I was a secret and I wouldn't want to ruin anyone's life." This just reinforced the feeling that my very existence was bad. I had very low self-esteem, and married the first guy who proposed because I was certain that no one else would ever want me. After all, if your parents don't want you, how can anyone else want you? I am blessed to have just celebrated thirty-seven years of marriage. I must admit, though, that had I not had a tremendous fear of abandonment, I probably would not be able to say that. Marriage is hard work and it has not been without its highs and lows, but I was determined that I would not be left behind again. I found my mother through DNA matching with my aunt. Reunion brings its own set of challenges. I had searched for so long that I was sure I was prepared for whatever it brought. Boy, was I wrong. No one can ever be prepared for reunion.

Ethnicity: White
Gender: Female
Current Age: Fifty-seven years old
Age of Adoption: One year and ten months old
Place of Birth: Baltimore, Maryland
Closed or Open Adoption: Closed

JOURNEY OF A LIFETIME

"Life is a journey that must be traveled no matter how bad the roads and accommodations."

Oliver Goldsmith

It's very hard for me to define adoption. Each member of the triad stands from a different viewpoint. As a foster parent and an adoptive parent myself, I am keenly aware of how different the perspectives are. However, when broken down to its very simplest form for the sake of a definition, adoption is the relinquishing of one family through choice, termination, or coercion to create or add to another family.

My earliest memory associated with being adopted is from preschool. Our class had a young boy come to our school to share about his disability. He was born without legs, and proceeded to show us the tools and prosthetics he used. I found it fascinating and it was also my first exposure to someone with disabilities. However, at some point after that presentation, a teacher suggested to me that I should share about my adoption. Immediately, within my four-year-old brain, the connection was made in my head that I was different, just like that boy with no legs. I was other.

One question I get asked frequently about my own adoption is "Am I grateful?" My instinctual response to this is, "Am I grateful that I was given up for adoption? Absolutely not." Yes, many adoptees love their adoptive parents and lives. We are grateful. However, those lives are based upon the foundation that we were initially abandoned, rejected, or lost through termination by our biological parents or family. That foundation of abandonment was the most difficult part of being adopted. Rejection and the fear of it seeped into every aspect and facet of my life. Back then, little was known about separation trauma and how that affects the physiology of a person. Even now as an adult adoptee, having gone through trauma therapy, the fear of rejection still makes attempts to permeate my life, my decisions, and my relationships.

It is this fear of rejection that used to control my actions and infiltrate my relationships. Driven and steered through the lens of the fear of rejection, I was self-destructive and self-sabotaging in my life choices. "There is something wrong with [her]," became an echo that followed behind me, spoken by teachers, administrators, youth leaders, and even friends and their parents. I walked on unstable ground, around everyone and in everything, fearing that the floor would fall out from beneath me at any moment. It was not until I was thirty-four years old, in one of my foster parent trainings, that I heard the word "trauma" uttered. That word changed the trajectory of my life, and I am on my way to healing. As an adoptive parent, I have learned that it is vital for adoptive parents to first deal with their own trauma and baggage before even entering into the adoption process. It is also vital to listen to the voice of adult adoptees as the experts, and to continue to learn and educate oneself on adoption and the issues their children will face. Finally, they must never assume that an adopted child is not dealing with something or won't deal with an adoptee issue simply because they haven't spoken about it, shown signs of it, or seem to be well-rounded. Healing from being adopted is a journey and will take an entire lifetime.

Ethnicity: White
Gender: Female
Current Age: Thirty-seven years old
Age of Adoption: Three days old
Place of Birth: Southfield, Michigan
Closed or Open Adoption: Open

TWO FAMILIES

"We have two families in life. One we're born with that shares our blood. Another we meet along the way that's willing to give its life for us."

Mark Frost

Overall, being adopted has been a blessing. I knew from a very young age that I was adopted. My adoptive parents were very open and very supportive. I always knew I was different, my adoptive mom was white with red hair and freckles, and we looked nothing alike. At a young age, people would see me standing with her and approach me and ask me where was my mother.

My adoption didn't start to affect my life until I got older and lost both of my adoptive parents. I went through an extremely depressed stage. Being adopted has caused abandonment issues that will never go away.

I found my biological family in 2012. It was a wonderful reunion, and I was welcomed with open arms. After having my first child, I believe God gave me two families for a reason and I am so grateful to have blessed my adoptive parents lives the way they blessed me.

Ethnicity: Black
Gender: Female
Current Age: Twenty-nine years old
Age of Adoption: Birth
Place of Birth: Detroit, Michigan
Closed or Open Adoption: Closed

WHERE DO I BELONG?

"Not belonging is a terrible feeling. It feels awkward and it hurts, as if you were wearing someone else's shoes."

Phoebe Stone

Adoption to me is taking someone into your life to love, hold, and nurture. In my earliest memory of my adoption, I was around four years old and I remember being happy that my aunt and uncle had taken me in to give me a new life. But that is where the happiness ends ... and the questions begin.

Where do I fit in? That is the question I have asked myself a hundred times over the past ten years. My adoption took place in 1987 between my birth family (Pam and George) and my aunt and uncle (Jackson and Lynn). Growing up, I knew I was adopted and I was fine with it. Until my birth mom started dating a man and started raising his two-year-old daughter, Melanie.

It then made me wonder why I was not good enough, what had I done wrong to be given away for a $1000 and a trailer? Granted, it was totally illegal, but the facts are just that. Personally, I think a closed adoption would have been a lot better. Adoption outside of my immediate family, so I wouldn't have to question why I wasn't good enough to keep.

Jackson and Lynn raised me, but even there I never felt welcome after reaching my teenage years and wanting to find out where I was from. Extended family never accepted me as a member of the family. My biological family and I do not mesh well, and I keep my distance. I figured with time I would heal, instead I find myself wondering *how, why, and what if?* At age thirty-five, I am still left wondering, *where do I fit in? Where is my place in the world? Where is my family? Where do I belong? One family found me worthless, the other never fully accepted me, so where in the world do I belong?*

Ethnicity: White
Gender: Female
Current Age: Thirty-seven years old
Age of adoption: Two and a half years old
Place of Birth: Kingsport, Tennessee
Closed or Open Adoption: Open

THE PROCESS

"We should work on our process, not the outcome of our processes."

W. Edwards Deming

Adoption is a term that I believe is weighted toward the adoptive parents. It describes the process of people choosing to take in and raise a child to whom they are not biologically related. However, the word adoption says nothing about the first stage of the process: the biological parents' relinquishing of the child. Sadly, that stage of the process is most often minimized or ignored, which I believe does the adopted child a great disservice.

My adoptive parents followed the accepted practice and told me I was adopted as early as possible, as soon as they thought I could grasp the concept. I think that was a good thing, because it normalized my status ... at least it did for a few years.

When I was ten, my teacher tasked me to write an essay. I wrote mine on adoption. When I handed it in, she brought her hand to her cheek and exclaimed, "Oh, my! I didn't know you were adopted!" I felt like she just discovered I had some sort of disease that should have been previously divulged, like epilepsy. That was the first time I felt that maybe I should keep my adoption status to myself.

Now that I'm an adult, I would say the most difficult aspect of being adopted is not feeling as if I fit in anywhere. I didn't fit in with my adoptive family. My adoptive father was a mason contractor who liked to play golf. I was a sensitive, artistic type who enjoyed drawing and music. By age seven or eight, he seemed to lose interest in me. My adoptive mother was a narcissist with borderline personality disorder and an addiction to amphetamines. I endured a great deal of emotional abuse from her.

My mother said a lot of horrible things to me, but I think the worst was, "Do you like your ears? Because we could save up to get you plastic surgery." Or, "You should get a perm so your hair can be curlier [like hers]." I suspect she was trying to remold me in her image.

I reunited with my birth family, I searched and found my birth mother in 1991, and we had a reunion in 1992. Birth mother told me who my birth father was, and I sought him out and met him a year or so later. In early 2019, I took a DNA test and discovered that the man my mother told me was my father was not. I sought out my actual birth father, who had passed away, so I contacted his widow.

When I found my birth mother, I wondered if I would become close to her and her family, thinking our shared DNA might magically knit us together, but that was not to be. I wondered if I would have been a black sheep had I grown up with my biological family. Or was it simply that time and distance had severed those bonds beyond repair?

I certainly had more opportunities with my adoptive family. They were a bit more affluent than my biological family. They knew how to give me things. Sadly, they did not know how to give of themselves.

If I were to give advice to prospective adoptive parents, it would be to do what it takes to minimize your own insecurities so you can embody the uniqueness and differences of adopted children. Help them feel accepted unconditionally just as they are. Let them know they belong.

Ethnicity: White
Gender: Male
Current Age: Sixty-one years old
Age of Adoption: Birth
Place of Birth: Encino, California
Closed or Open Adoption: Closed

DÉJÀ VU

"There's an expression, déjà vu, that means that you feel like you've been somewhere before, that you've somehow already dreamed it or experienced it in your mind."

Neil Gaiman

I was adopted from South Korea to Sweden when I was almost six years old, so I remember things that probably a regular child should not have remembered. I lived in poverty and experienced heavy mental and physical abuse from my Korean father and other relatives. My Korean mother was powerless at that time, and couldn't help my little brother or me.

We both ended up being put up for adoption. I was sad, angry, and disappointed at my Korean mother as a child. I couldn't understand why my own mother didn't love me. As you can guess, I was a troubled kid. It didn't make it easier when I quickly found out that my new adoptive family wasn't what I expected. By that time, a kid like me needed a lot of love and attention. However, this new family had another family member who was mentally abusive, and relatives who chose to stay blind. Déjà vu all over again. This made it harder for me to find inner peace. Luckily, at an early age I found peace in reading books (especially fantasy books), painting, dance, music, and other creative arts. It also helped me with controlling my emotions and staying occupied.

As an adult, traveling has been another important piece of my personal growth. At the age of twenty-four, I chose to go back to South Korea to live and find answers to my questions. I reunited with my Korean mother, who is now remarried to an adorable man. When I heard her version of the story, it made me more peaceful, because now I could understand why.

Today, ironically, I'm partly experiencing a déjà vu again, but as an adult and in the United States, the third country I have lived in.

This time I can understand more quickly what's going on with myself emotionally. I have learned that when you don't feel any unconditional love, combined with misunderstandings, you also become emotionally unstable. I do believe it's more common among adoptees. Perhaps because we feel lost and we are stuck in between where we are now and where we came from. Love is truly the most powerful tool humans have. Adoptees, it's time to love ourselves.

Ethnicity: Korean
Gender: Female
Current Age: Thirty-three years old
Age of Adoption: Almost six years old
Place of Birth: South Korea
Closed or Open Adoption: Closed

POSITIVE LIGHT

"I always like to look on the optimistic side of life, but I am realistic enough to know that life is a complex matter. "

Walt Disney

I have always looked at adoption in a positive light. I have always viewed it as a second chance to grow up in a nurtured and healthy household. I love my adoptive parents. I am so grateful they are in my life. I honestly could not imagine growing up and not having them in my life. Adoption has allowed me to see the world in a less linear way than my counterparts. Because I am Asian and my parents are White, I have always seen the world in a different and more complex way than someone who is not adopted. I find that a gift. It has taught me that family comes in many different shapes and forms and that as long as love, support, and happiness are found, that is what creates a strong family unit. However, growing up in the Midwest and being one of the very few Asians in my hometown, it was difficult to fit in and feel like I meshed with the community sometimes. But now I am proud to be a Korean adoptee, because it has made me a more compassionate, caring, and understanding person in my life. I do not think I have ever been asked a question about my adoption that I found offensive. Usually when I have brought it up in the past, I would only get positive feedback and genuine interest in my life story. I feel lucky in that sense. My best advice that I would give to an adoptive parent or perspective adoptive parent is to know what you are getting yourself into and to make sure you always give as much love, support, and kindness to your adopted child as you can. They are going through a lot as it is, and they will need your constant love and support throughout their lifetime.

Ethnicity: Korean
Gender: Female
Current Age: Twenty-eight years old

Age of Adoption: Four months old
Place of Birth: Chungcheongbuk-do, South Korea
Closed or Open Adoption: Closed (International)

LATE DISCOVERY

"There are no secrets that time does not reveal."

Jean Racine

Adoption has ruined my life in a lot of ways. I found out at twenty-two that I was adopted, and ever since then I have felt lost and alone in life. There is no relationship anymore with any family. I feel lost and alone, and doubt I will ever recover and will always feel alone.

Ethnicity: White
Sex: Male
Current Age: Thirty-three years old
Age of Adoption: Birth
Place of Birth: Ireland
Closed or Open Adoption: Closed

ADOPTION ON FILM

"When you stand and share your story in an empowering way, your story will heal you and your story will heal someone else."

Iyanla Vanzant

Adoption for me, personally, has been a life-long journey. It has colored my life in both positive and negative ways. While I have loving parents who raised me in middle-class America, it did not protect me from the trauma I experienced from the loss of my first family, foster family, birth country, and culture. The way trauma manifested within me has left life-long struggles that I continue to deal with even as an adult. Growing up, I struggled with separation anxiety, self-worth, a sense of belongingness, and not feeling loved enough. Even today, there are traces of what I felt so strongly as a child and I still have nightmares of people that I love leaving me.

I was fortunate that my parents created a safe and open environment for me to talk about my emotions and feelings about anything challenging in my life, including adoption. The empathy I remember my mother showing as I shared what was in my heart with her truly made all the difference in allowing us to have a close relationship with one another. For a long time, I thought all adoptive families had parents like mine. But I learned in my late teens that many adoptees didn't have that open dialogue with their adoptive parents and it caused deep rifts in their relationships.

The first time I told my story on camera, about meeting my first mother and aunt at seventeen, was for a high school documentary. It was a very healing experience for me and I knew that, as a creative film-maker, I one day wanted to help others share their adoption experience on this unique platform, not only to help in their paths of healing, but also to help others who might benefit from hearing their stories. That day came after a devastating breakup occurred, which triggered trauma related to my adoption, when I needed to revisit the dreams I had set aside. I realized it was time to stop adapting myself to the needs and wants of others to keep their love and acceptance, even at the expense of my own well-being, for fear of being rejected. Re-discovering my passion for creating a space for people to tell their stories through the video lens has been an incredible journey. I continue to gain insight through this process, and learn new things about myself I didn't know were there.

Ethnicity: Korean
Gender: Female
Current Age: Thirty-six years old
Age of Adoption: Eleven months old
Place of Birth: Outside of Seoul, Korea
Closed or Open Adoption: Closed (International)

SUFFERING IN SILENCE

"The deepest pain I ever felt was denying my own feelings to make everyone else comfortable."

Nicole Lyons

Growing up, no one truly asked me how I felt about my own adoption. I guess you could say I suffered in silence. No one ever wants to talk about the loss. They expect you to pretend like nothing ever happened. And that is what hurts the most.

Ethnicity: Black
Gender: Female
Current Age: Thirty-seven years old
Age of Adoption: Six weeks old
Place of Birth: New Orleans, Louisiana
Closed or Open Adoption: Closed

Now it's your turn. Reflect on your own adoption experience. In what ways has adoption affected your life?

Ethnicity:
Sex:
Current Age:
Age of Adoption:
Place of Birth:
Closed or Open Adoption:

ABOUT THE AUTHORS

Veronica Breaux was born in New Orleans, Louisiana, through the closed adoption system. While searching for her own birth family, she began to meet others in the adoption community and began to realize how significantly adoption had an impact on her own life. She graduated with a bachelor of arts degree in sociology from The University of New Orleans in 2005 and later went on to earn a master's degree in mental health counseling from Webster University in 2013. Veronica is currently a registered intern counselor with the state of Florida. She hopes that she can help educate adoptive parents and others in the counseling profession on adoption-related trauma and be an advocate for other adoptees. Veronica believes no one should be denied the right to know who he or she is. In her spare time, she enjoys baking, cooking, photography, traveling, and, for the first time ever, genealogy research.

Shelby Kilgore is an adoptee from Korea and has been producing reality/documentary series for the past fifteen years, after graduating from The University of Florida with a bachelor's degree in telecommunications in 2006. As an adoptee from Korea, Shelby first told her adoption story on camera when she was seventeen. It was a very healing experience for her, and she knew one day she would help others tell their stories. Once Shelby became an established producer, with two Daytime Emmy wins under her belt, she became confident enough to start her passion project of spreading education and awareness about foster care and adoption through the video lens. In 2012, she filmed her first interviews and launched her YouTube Channel: Shelby Redfield Kilgore and Facebook page: Adoption Awareness. You can find all of her work at wearemirrorlight.com. Reading is one of her favorite things to do, as well as singing and traveling around the world.

Veronica and Shelby can be contacted at rootedinadoption@gmail.com.